Author

David Bouchard, speaker, author and educator is an award winning writer who has penned over 70 books in both English and French. David is one of Canada's most sought after public speakers for his gift of storytelling. In 2009 he was named to the Order of Canada for his contribution as an author of children's books. David is Métis/Ojibway of the Martin Clan, his Ojibway name is Zhiibaayaanakwad. Born and raised in Saskatchewan, David now lives in Victoria, B.C

www.davidbouchard.com

Artist

Kristy Cameron, is a teacher, and artist who was born and raised in northwestern Ontario. Growing-up surrounded by the beauty of the natural world has given her endless subjects to paint. Kristy is a well-known artist who has collaborated in the past with writer David Bouchard, providing beautiful illustrations for his books including Seven Sacred Teachings. Kristy is of Métis descent and still lives in her hometown of Atikokan, Ontario Canada.

www.kristycameron.ca

"For my daughter Victoria. I dreamed that you would grow knowing your family, and my dream has come true."

Meet Your Family has been retold as Gikenim Giniigi'igoog
from the Ojibwe worldview and perspective.
As each language is unique in its delivery of the story
the translation will not match word for word.

Project Manager: Teddy Anderson
Design: Eden Sunflower (MWE Staff)
Editor: Kaitlyn Stampflee (MWE Staff)
ISBN: 978-1-989122-66-2
For more book information go to www.medicinewheel.education

Funded by the
Government
of Canada

Financé par le
gouvernement
du Canada

Meet Your Family

Gikenim Giniigi'igoog

David Bouchard

Paintings by Kristy Cameron

As Told in Ojibwe by
Jason & Nancy Jones

Meet Your Mother
Gikenim Gimaamaa

We all come from her
Those with feathers or fur
Those who walk on two legs
Birthed from water or eggs

Those with leaves or with thorns
Those with fins or with horns
Those with fingers and thumbs
All from her — everyone

She birthed and she feeds us
Protects and provides us
With clothes and with shelter
From harsh, dangerous weather

She's the grass on the prairie
The leaves that will shade me
The lakes and the mountains
Whose waters make fountains

She's the tree in the forest
The meadow before it
She is where we are from
All from her — everyone

Meet Your Father
Gikenim Gidede

Look up, see that blue
He's there looking at you
He's your Father the Sky
If you care to know why

You can see him up there
He's the guardian who cares
Both your Father and mine
He's been there for all time

He's the giver of breath
From your time in the nest
He's the bringer of light
From the darkness of night

Meet Your Grandfather
Gikenim Gimishoomis

We learn from the Sun
He makes learning fun
Shows us just how to live
When to take — when to give

He warms up our Mother
Empowers our Father
Provides us each day
With a safe place to play

We follow his lead
As we learn to fight greed
Watch him move through the sky
Learning how, when and why

And we watch him go round
From our place on the ground
It's from him up above
That we learn how to love

Meet Your Grandmother
Gikenim Gookomis

She's there every night
Up there in full sight
She lights up the way
Until night turns to day

She cares for our Father
Provides for our Mother
Through her comes rebirth
And new life to the earth

And although I can't see
Her back, they see me
Been there for all time
Mine and yours, yours and mine

To help us keep track
We use turtle's back
The shapes there will show
What should come or should go

All Our Relations
Gidiniwemaaganaanig

Look back at the sky
For truth, you know why
You've learned from the Sun
That all — we are one

The earth is your Mother
The tree is your brother
So too are the swimmers
The lakes and the rivers

The birds in the sky
The worm and the fly
Four-leggeds and snakes
The fish in the lakes

Now look at the stars
Do you know who they are
Our relations look down
At those still on the ground

www.medicinewheel.education

Online Courses Available:
www.classroom.medicinewheel.education

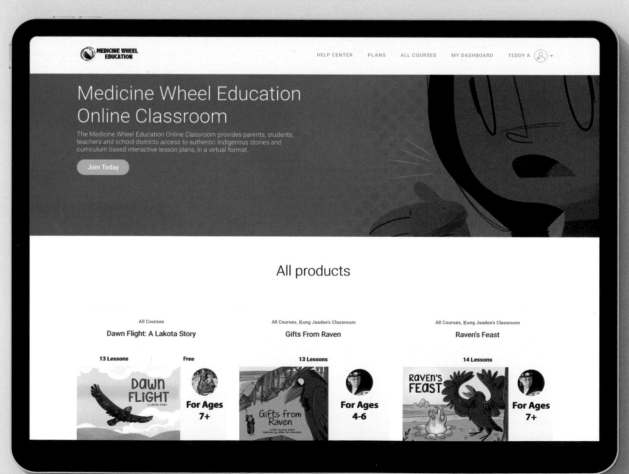

We Learn from the Sun

David Bouchard
Paintings by Kristy Cameron

Rencontre ta famille
Gikenim Giniigi'igoog

David Bouchard
Illustrations par Kristy Cameron
Tel que raconté en langue ojibwée par
Jason & Nancy Jones

THIS IS WHAT
I'VE BEEN TOLD
MII YE GAA-BE-WIINDMAAGOOYAANG

WRITTEN & ILLUSTRATED BY
CHERYL ARMSTRONG

The Eagle Feather

Written By Kevin Locke
Illustrated by Jessika von Innerebner

Trudy's Healing
Stone

Written by Trudy Spiller
Illustrated by Jessika von Innerebner

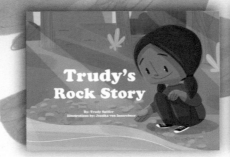

Trudy's
Rock Story

By: Trudy Spiller
Illustrations by: Jessika von Innerebner

The Orange Shirt Story

Author: Phyllis Webstad
Illustrations: Brock Nicol

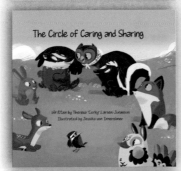

The Circle of Caring and Sharing

Written by Theresa 'Corky' Larsen-Jonasson
Illustrated by Jessika von Innerebner

The Hoop Dancer's
Teachings

Written by Teddy Anderson
Illustrated by Jessika von Innerebner

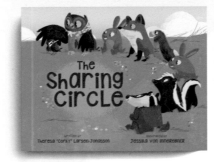

THE
SHARING
CIRCLE

Written by Theresa "Corky" Larsen-Jonasson
Illustrated by Jessika von Innerebner

DAWN
FLIGHT
A LAKOTA STORY

WRITTEN BY KEVIN LOCKE   ILLUSTRATED BY JESSIKA VON INNEREBNER

Gifts from
Raven

Written by Kung Jaadee
Illustrated by Jessika von Innerebner

Phyllis's Orange
Shirt

Written by Phyllis Webstad
Illustrated by Brock Nicol

RAVEN'S
FEAST

BY KUNG JAADEE   ILLUSTRATED BY JESSIKA VON INNEREBNER

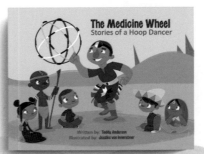

The Medicine Wheel
Stories of a Hoop Dancer

Written by: Teddy Anderson
Illustrated by: Jessika von Innerebner